F*CK!
I'M IN MY
TWENTIES

emma koenig

CHRONICLE BOOKS
SAN FRANCISCO

Library of Congress Cataloging-in-Publication Data:

Koenig, Emma.

 F*CK! : I'm in my twenties / Emma Koenig.

   p. cm.

 ISBN 978-1-4521-1053-0

 1. Young adults--Humor. 2. Adulthood--Humor. I. Title.

 PN6231.A26K64 2012

 818'.602--dc23

                    2012006877

ISBN: 978-1-4521-1053-0

Manufactured in North America

Designed by Emily Dubin

10 9 8 7 6 5 4

Chronicle Books LLC
680 Second Street
San Francisco, California 94107
www.chroniclebooks.com

For my parents.
I FUCKING LOVE YOU!

FUCK!

The day I turned twenty, everything changed and the world drained of its color. A dark storm cloud settled atop my head, raining down furiously every time I attempted to get out of bed. I was taunted by melancholy music, which attacked me from every direction, crawling into my ears and burrowing into the folds of my cerebral cortex. I soldiered on, the odious orchestra delving deeper into the dungeon of my being until it invaded my heart.

Okay. Well. Not really. It wasn't (completely) like that. Maybe I wasn't outfitted with my own personal rain cloud, but something weird was at play. I had entered into uncharted territory. But I am getting ahead of myself. Let me begin at the beginning. Or at least in the same general area as where the beginning would be if I were any good at reflecting upon life in a super-linear fashion.

Around the time I began my junior year in college, I began hearing a lot of cautionary tales from friends who were older than I and already out. All of them got the same kind of faraway look in their eyes as they warned me about the impending hopelessness and depression that would inevitably wreak havoc upon my life.

"You're so lucky that you're still in school," they'd say wistfully, with just a hint of contempt. Then the tone of the conversation would shift, and it was as if these friends and I were on a sinking ship in remote and stormy waters in the Pacific and there was only one more seat on the rescue boat and they were dying of cholera and we had already eaten the other crew members and it began to make sense for me to leave them and save myself. With voices that practically leaped out of their throats and gripped my forearm like the claws of a panther, they would say, "STAY IN SCHOOL AS LONG AS YOU CAN."

However, since I was still a raging optimist at that point, the claws felt more like the playful tickle of a kitten's paws. "Okay, okay, my little kitty-witty," I'd say in a baby voice, "Let's not get too excited. Mommy's going to be just fine."

Clearly I assumed that these harrowing accounts of the slings and arrows of the real world did not apply to me. The chances of me waking up with a missing kidney in a bathtub full of ice seemed more likely than the idea of being severely unhappy after I graduated.

Alas, fast-forwarding about a year, I found myself saying horrifyingly similar phrases to people who were maybe six months younger than I, just like some clichéd after-school special wherein the one belief that the protagonist decries becomes the bane of her existence. "APPRECIATE YOUR TIME IN COLLEGE! ENJOY IT WHILE IT LASTS!" I'd bellow to anyone standing within ten feet of me.

How did this happen?? How did I join the ranks of the postcollege disenchanted? Perhaps it came down to my tragic character flaw, the inability to live in the moment. When I was in middle school, I wanted to be in high school. When I was in high school, I wanted to be in college. When I was in college, I wanted to be starting my career. Once I got there, I just wanted to get beyond Phase I: The Shitty Years, and on to Phase II: When All My Dreams Come True ASAP. I could have sworn that during freshman orientation the dean had said that as soon as we got our diplomas, a genie would appear and grant infinite wishes. Although now that I think of it, I may have misheard her because I was texting. Plus, I thought that having my BFA would eliminate the necessity of continuing to pay any more dues because they would have been paid in full by my spending almost my entire life thus far as a student. Now I have

to consider that maybe that guy in the subway who always yells, "College is a lie!" knows what he's talking about.

Yes, boys and girls, I've come to see that everything I thought I knew about Phase II was wrong. Very wrong. Oh, how wrong I was. Have I mentioned that I had some misconceptions about Phase II?

I had even graduated a semester early so I could get a head start on (hating) my life! At that point, I felt completely ready to pick up my all-access pass to Easy Street. Right out of the gate, it seemed like I had a bright future ahead of me! I had a steady job with flexible hours (as a coat check girl, getting paid only in tips), a cool St. Marks Place apartment (with a bedroom ten inches larger than my bed on all sides and inhabited by mice who were evidently genetically resistant to poison), an exciting love life (hooking up with someone who was evidently genetically resistant to a relationship), a kick-ass social life (where no one had time for each other because they were so busy going batshit crazy with their own lives), and a shimmering, glimmering dream: "I am going to be an actor!" (in a tampon commercial . . . if I'm really lucky).

Sounds totes awesome, right? In no short order, the fantasy was beginning to crumble all around me, and I was sinking deeper and deeper into the quicksand of post-collegiate life. How had I been able to romanticize the real world right up to the moment I was living in it?

Maybe part of the problem was that I tended to have a hard time thinking in realistic terms. For example, I had always regarded Los Angeles as a concept, a slide show of images from pop culture: palm trees, fake boobs, people with frightening tans. When I finally visited LA for the first time last year, I had to concede that LA actually existed; people really did live there. Similarly, it took me a long time to recognize that being in my twenties had also existed as a concept that didn't match up with reality. I'm not sure if I expected Mayor Bloomberg to give me a key to the city (seriously, do those get you into every single apartment? Just asking . . . for a friend.), but I certainly didn't expect to have Mr. Guinness himself letting me know that I had broken the world record for Most Meltdowns in a Single Week.

The truth is that graduating from college is just like any other landmark rite of passage, like, say, losing one's virginity. In anticipation of that event, we can only hypothesize based on preliminary "bases" run, what friends tell us/ lie about, and what we see in movies like *Ernest Goes to Camp* and *Interview with a Vampire*. Then, when it actually happens, isn't it usually just the simple awareness of being in that moment? It isn't so scary or crazy, it just kind of is. "So . . . I am having sex now." When it happened to me I certainly felt more complete and adult from the experience, but it's not like I suddenly got any superpowers, like I could communicate with the dead (which would have been nifty, although after a week or so, it would have probably become quite stressful).

However, what I anticipated happening to me when I graduated from college was the equivalent of becoming the Pink Power Ranger (Viva l'Amy Jo Johnson!). I imagined that even the most basic of tasks, like walking down a flight of stairs, would be exhilarating and joyous because I had a college degree! Instead, I found out that the accumulated impressions from past experiences, others' reports, and media representations did not fully prepare me for the WTF-ness of actually living it. "So . . . I'm in my twenties now." And it really sucks.

Dealing with the all the anti-fanfare was crowding the space in my brain. I hated that almost every conversation I had was either a defensive explanation of my life or a bland packaged script; both were devices to prove to whomever I was addressing that I had everything under control. Which I most definitely did not. I also couldn't tell if I was overreacting. Was everyone else pleased as punch with their twenties? Was I insane for experiencing it this way? Did my mother obsessively read *The Bell Jar* when I was in utero? WHAT WAS WRONG WITH ME?

I found that one of the only things that kept me sane was talking to people who were going through the same thing. What a relief to discover that most of the people I knew were also dealing with the waking fever dream of unsatisfactory apartment/job/friends/love/life/career goals. Everyone had something to complain about, and we engaged in a lot of kvetching sessions.

Having gone to drama school, where it's a prerequisite to have taken Overanalyzing 101 and to carry a Moleskine notebook everywhere, I found myself notating the issues my friends and I discussed, whether they were epiphanies or regrets or explanations or questions.

Documenting my problems allowed me to see the sublime in the disappointing.

Thus, *Fuck! I'm in My Twenties* was hatched. I had originally planned on only sharing it with friends, but shortly after I put it online, it took on a life of its own, and has brought us to this moment: you holding this book in your hands! This isn't a "how-to" book or a "how-not-to" book, it's more of a "how do I deal with my life without wanting to stab myself in the eyes with icicles?" book.

Now some of you may say, "Just get over it, Emma. Nobody cares." To those people, I say, "OH, REALLY? IS THAT SO?" I mean, sure, maybe you have a point. And maybe I need to work on wittier retorts. Perhaps you're one of those people who is (or was) perfectly content in your twenties. If so, FUCK YOU! I mean, um, CONGRATS, but bro, have some compassion for those of us who have not reached the enlightenment phase yet. What are you, an animal?!

I don't think anyone has truly "figured out" being in his or her twenties until, at the very least, they're in their thirties and have reached the analysis/justification phase of what has transpired over the previous decade. Or perhaps it's not that way at all, and my thirties will be another elusive concept that I won't have mastered until I'm forty. I haven't gotten very far at all imagining what my thirties will be like, except for owning a really nice desk lamp. My poorly constructed idea definitely needs to be fleshed out, and it may take quite a bit of time because right now most of my brain is under construction.

Now for the cheesy part. At the beginning of college I attended a talk given by Oskar Eustis, the artistic director of the Public Theater in New York City. He said, "As artists, we make contracts to care about each other's work." At the time I was awestruck to hear that part of being an artist is supporting other artists, that community is inextricably linked with individual creative work. As human beings, we also must make contracts to give a shit about each other. It's easy to be selfish in your twenties because you have to be concerned with your own life and taking the right steps toward being a real adult, but you have to find a balance between blazing your own trail and being there for your friends. You make it harder for yourself if you only care about yourself.

Also, not to get all nouveau-hippie on you, but there is a reason that in a yoga class you are constantly reminded to keep breathing. Breathing itself may be an involuntary action, but when your body encounters something difficult, you start to hold your breath. The same thing is true in life. Sometimes, until it is pointed out, you forget to fully breathe. That is why we need to remind ourselves and our friends to support each other, keep breathing, and to enjoy the fuck out of our young lives!

I remain on my quest to make sense of it all even if everything I say now will embarrass me once I'm out of my twenties. I hope that my attempt to figure it out will remind all of you that you're not alone.

WHAT IT FEELS LIKE TO BE IN YOUR TWENTIES

explanation attempt #1

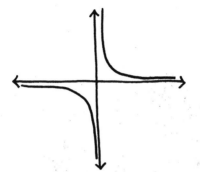

infinitely
approaching
zero

Ideas for how to respond when someone asks what you do: (when you're in your 20s and aren't living UNDERLINE YOUR DREAM yet)

- "I've gotten really into licking dirty surfaces"

- vomit on their shoes and then ~~profusely apologize~~ DO NOT APOLOGIZE!

- "I'm volunteering at a Tamagotchi pet shelter"

- "I've been breaking my back trying to get into the porn game, but all the casting is super political and I don't have the aptitude for DP, which put me at a disadvantage"

- give them a huge smile and then mime that you're trapped in a box and trying to escape

Craigslist

jobs

positions you're overqualified for

positions you're underqualified for

positions you're qualified for that you won't get

positions you're qualified for that won't pay enough

positions that will embarrass you

positions where your boss will be half your age and/or possess half your IQ

positions where you'll be paid under the table

positions that will demolish your social life

positions that will drive you insane and inspire intense homicidal fantasies

HAPPY   JOB   HUNTING!

COVER LETTER

Dear Person I Don't Know,

I am fucking great! At least that's what I tell myself to keep from drowning in self hatred. Please validate my existence by offering me a job.

Please see attached resume.

Sincerely (at least somewhat),
Me
Me

REAL RESUME

PROCRASTINATION & AVOIDANCE   2004 - Present
- Responsibilities include NOT DOING an array of tasks, ranging from simple errands (i.e. not depositing checks, not doing laundry, + not picking up prescriptions) to more intellectually and emotionally complex undertakings (i.e. not confronting people, not being honest with myself, + being able to achieve a total denial of reality).

APPLYING LIQUID EYELINER   2002 - Present
- Fearless use of black liquid liner in high pressure situations, despite risks involved with failure to properly apply

MAKING MYSELF THROW UP WHEN I'VE DRUNK TOO MUCH   2006 - Present
- Ability to pull the trigger and remove toxic material from body while maintaining some semblance of dignity.

FELLATIO   2005 - Present
- Expertise due to unique blend of: outrageous amounts of Cosmo articles read, free online porn watched, and hands-on experiences accumulated. References available upon request.

BUYING GROCERIES I NEVER EAT   2006 - Present
- Adherence to misguided belief that if money is invested in food, said food will be prepared and consumed.

EDUCATION: Prestigious/ Pretentious Art School

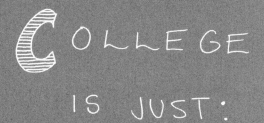

COLLEGE

IS JUST:

SHOWING
PEOPLE
YOUTUBE
VIDEOS

COMPARING
REGIONAL
SLANG AND
DIALECTS

Pop?! You mean soda?
Do you say "roof" like "ruff"??
Hold on. It's "bagel," not "begel." It's a long "a" sound.
Now I can't remember if I say it like "ORange" or "ARange"!
Let me show you a video that I think is SUPER FUNNY and you will find KINDA FUNNY!
Yayyyy!

graduation goody bag:

THE COMPLETE IDIOT'S GUIDE TO JOBS IN THE FOODSERVICE INDUSTRY

TISSUES

Perfect for your tri-daily sobbing spells about the economic value of your BFA!

Prozac® 20mg

Free trial sample!

CONGRATS GRAD!

Drink away your sorrows in style with this commemorative flask!

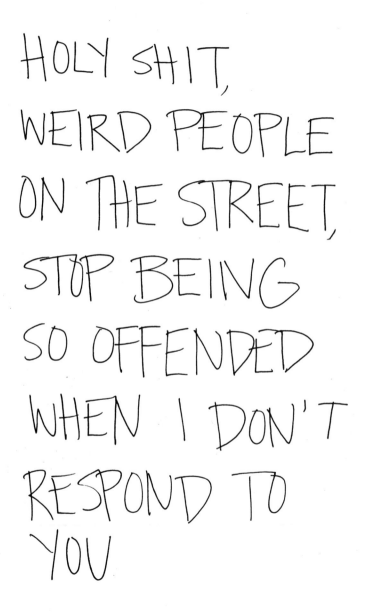

If I am < the person I'm talking to, I'm probably playing up what I'm doing with my life

---

If I am > the person I'm talking to, I'm probably downplaying what I'm doing with my life

---

If I am = the person I'm talking to, then hopefully I'm keeping it real

---

But no matter which angle I'm coming from, I'm trying to put the fact that

I DON'T HAVE WHAT I WANT YET

into a palatable package

I still can't let go of my superficial notions of what it means to be an adult:

a building with a doorman

regular size

obnoxiously large wine glasses

a long-term relationship

an extensive knowledge of wine

I'm good at communicating my feelings!

I'd like an earthy, robust red

a TV with fancy channels

SHOWTIME

being in the best shape of my life

Carrie Bradshaw-esque shoes that don't hurt

$500

zero stretch marks or cellulite

toned abs

thighs that don't touch

AT PRESS TIME, I POSSESS NONE OF THESE

WHAT IT FEELS LIKE TO BE IN YOUR TWENTIES

explanation attempt # 2

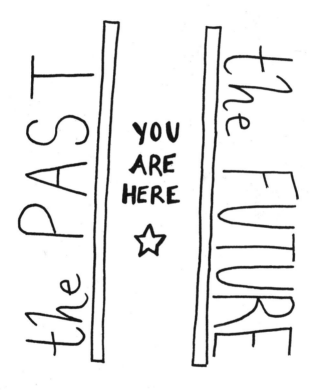

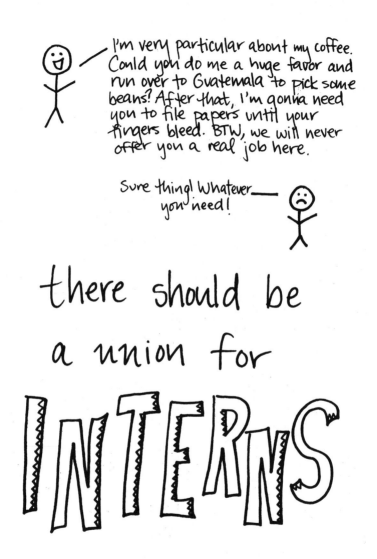

SPACE ALLOCATION GUIDELINES FOR MY BED

Edit Profile

Relationship Status:

- Single
- Desperately single
- In a relationship
- In a fragile relationship
- It's complicated
- It's super fucking complicated
- Kind of hooking up with someone
- Involved in something, but have no idea what to call it
- have no idea what I want
- No comment

when else
am I going
to sleep with
ALL THE
WRONG
PEOPLE?

Contacts List
Douchebag McGee
Do Not Pick Up
G-list Celeb From Bar
Frenemy
Pathological Liar
Don't Pick Up Fo Realzzz
Sketchy Drug Delivery Service
IF YOU PICK UP, YOU ARE ACCEPTING FULL RESPONSIBILITY FOR THE RICOCKULOUS SHITSTORM THAT IS ABOUT TO TAKE PLACE
Actual Friend

A date is like a job interview, but without:

GLOWING RECOMMENDATIONS FROM YOUR PAST

- "Down to earth!"
- "Passionate!"
- "Intellectual!"

RESUME OF RECENT IMPRESSIVE EXPLOITS

BEING ALLOWED TO CITE YOUR STRENGTHS AND WHY YOU'D BE A GOOD ASSET TO THE OTHER PERSON

ME! Cool shit about me!

"I'm confident in my ability to..."

Am I going through **puberty** all over again?

ANDROGENIC HAIR

I am growing hair in places I didn't even know were possible. Super.

HORMONES

How have I still not adjusted to this insane hormones roller coaster?

BODY SHAPE

Is it too late to reverse the damage of not sleeping and drinking cheap booze for the past decade? Is it??

ACNE

OK, cool, I am still breaking out. GREAT.

Typically, I have a strong penchant for

BREAKFAST SANDWICHES!!

no matter the circumstance. But when I'm hung<u>over</u>, I become very <u>entitled</u> about them.

"It is my god given right to be in possession of bacon, egg & cheese on a bagel right this instant. I totally deserve it because I voluntarily got incredibly drunk last night."

WHAT IT FEELS LIKE
TO BE IN YOUR TWENTIES

explanation attempt #3

■ JUST FRIENDS (supposedly zero attraction)

- "He's like my <u>brother</u>!"
- "She's like my <u>sister</u>!"

FRIENDS W/ EMOTIONAL BENEFITS

+ We call each other pet names, as a joke, of course

+ We mention how attractive the other is & have hugs that last too long

+ We cuddle in bed while watching "30 Rock" and joke about how we'll marry each other in ten years if we're both single

+ Lots of "friend sleepovers." Lots of close calls.

+ We made out one time last summer

FRIENDS W/ PHYSICAL BENEFITS

+ We fool around here and there, but it's no big deal

+ We get it on regularly, usually while intoxicated

+ "It's just for fun. Neither of us wants anything serious"

+ "I mean, it's like we're dating. We just aren't exclusive"

+ Why the fuck aren't we exclusive? (this thought sometimes leads to the end OR you end up ⮧)

■ IN A RELATIONSHIP

WHAT IS THE AGE CUTOFF FOR HANGING OUT NAKED WITH YOUR FRIENDS?

Falling Down The Rabbit Holes
OF THE INTERNET

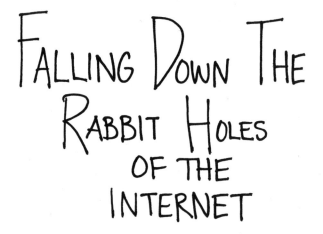

FACEBOOK

PORN

GOSSIP

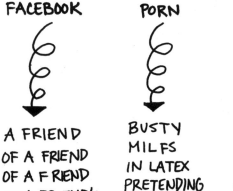

A FRIEND
OF A FRIEND
OF A FRIEND
OF A FRIEND'S
PROFILE

BUSTY
MILFS
IN LATEX
PRETENDING
TO BE
POLAR BEARS

D-LIST
CELEB'S
NIP SLIP
PIX FROM
3 DIFFERENT
ANGLES

WHY THE FUCK AM I LOOKING AT THIS SHIT!?

VENNTING

People I hang out with
People I'm facebook friends with
people who constantly invite me to their events
People who don't remember that not only have we previously met, but we are facebook friends

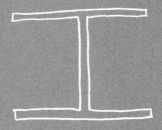

I
DO
NOT
RECOMMEND:

- trying to urinate into a small, decorative candle holder

- lending out almost anything you'd like to have back. it doesn't matter how trustworthy they seem, you will never see that "Wet Hot American Summer" DVD again

- thinking that doubling the recommended dose of medication will compensate for the fact that it's three years over the expiration date

- eating an elephantine amount of hot wings and mac & cheese from a questionable deli buffet at 3AM after a night of heavy drinking

- refusing to apologize out of pride

- being surrounded by 10 people who are on ecstasy and having the time of their lives when you are not on ecstasy

WHAT IT FEELS LIKE TO BE IN YOUR TWENTIES

explanation attempt #4

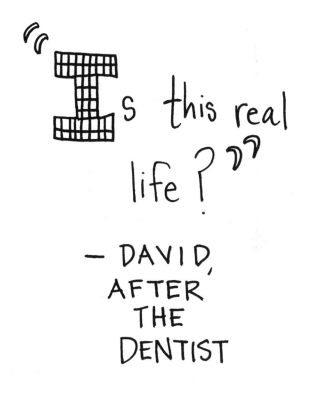

"Is this real life?"

— DAVID,
AFTER
THE
DENTIST

do you like me?
(check one)
YES
NO

are you going to stop liking me after you get what you want from me?
(check one)
YES
NO

DO NOT DISTURB

I just got home from a long day at work & I'm at the level of exhaustion where one's eyes involuntarily twitch. Additionally, the experiences I've accumulated today are contributing to my unparalleled resentment toward humanity. I just want to eat dinner in bed & look at pointless websites. If, despite my request, you decide to bother me, just know that I will hold it as a grudge for an indeterminate amount of time.

things I'd rather do than deal with apartment hunting, finding roommates, and all other aspects of moving:

- spend a year researching the textures of senior citizens' ears (with my tongue!)

- take the SATs every night

- snort lines of paprika off a VHS copy of Dustin Diamond's sex tape while being held hostage by a group of renegade nuns

- have an ambiguous liquid drip out of my belly button every time I get an email

- get a tattoo of all the hosts of "The View" that covers my entire face

Seriously, I would not wish the nightmare of moving upon my worst enemy

IS everyone ELSE actually HAPPIER than ME? or are they just better at PRETENDING?

It's a good idea to have a strong delivery of

"FUCK YOU!"

in your back pocket.

YOU NEVER KNOW WHEN YOU MIGHT NEED TO SHOUT THAT AT SOMEONE.

I recommend breathing from the diaphragm, speaking with conviction, and then running away as fast as possible so they don't beat you up.

TYPICAL CONVO: ACTOR EDITION

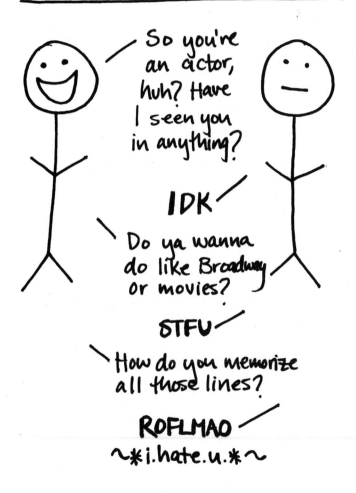

WHAT IT FEELS LIKE TO BE IN YOUR TWENTIES

explanation attempt #5

You do realize
that you're
BREAKING MY HEART,
right?

JUUUSSSST CHECKIIIINGGG!

Sex in High School:

Ah, <u>this</u> is what sex is like!

FAST ▷ ▷ FORWARD

Sex in Your Twenties:

Aaaahhh! <u>This</u>
is what
GOO<u>D</u> SEX
is like!

I STILL HAVEN'T FIGURED OUT HOW TO GET A DECENT NIGHT'S SLEEP NEXT TO SOMEONE I'M VERY ATTRACTED TO

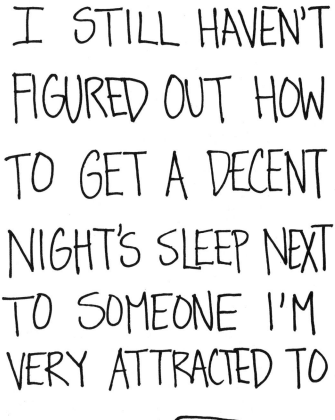

"GIVE
ME THE
BIGGEST
PIECE,
PLEASE!"

repeatedly biting off more
than I can chew

Moving Back In With Parents

DAY 1

This is the <u>best!</u> Clean sheets! Home-cooked meals! Help with my laundry! Just like a hotel!

DAY 20

Ok... so... the novelty is kind of starting to wear off.

DAY 45

FUCK. EVERYTHING. Somebody save me!

WHAT IT FEELS LIKE TO BE IN YOUR TWENTIES

explanation attempt #6

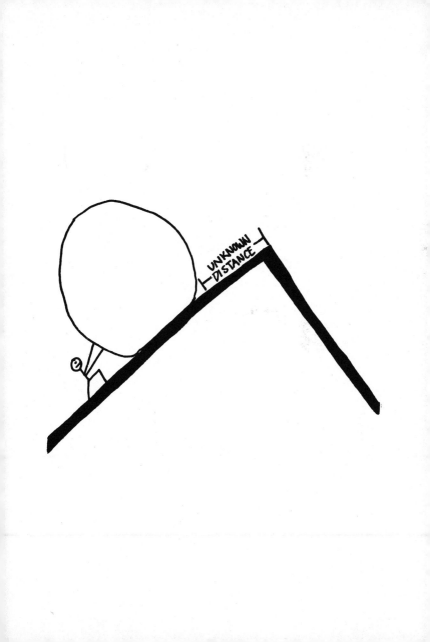

- getting walked in on in public bathrooms; anxiety is heightened when toilet is far from the door

- having my day job become my career

- two people I introduced becoming better friends with each other than they are with me

- knocking over a bottle in a liquor store and causing a domino effect

- never being able to pay my parents back what I owe them

- bad smell by proxy, particularly when walking through NYC in summer

- meeting the love of my life when there is a hickey on my neck

- total, absolute, 100% FAILURE

there are only so many
precautionary measures
you can take. sooner or later,
you are
going to get
hurt

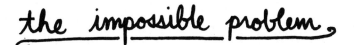

the impossible problem,

SOLVE FOR X & Y

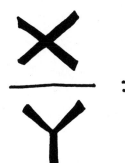 $= \dfrac{\text{time spent by myself}}{\text{time spent with others}}$

I can never find the right ratio

I always hit a point where
I become dissatisfied
with
TOO MUCH or too little
of either.

Did
COLLEGE
actually happen
or
was it just
a
strange dream I
had?

Did
HIGH SCHOOL
actually happen
or
was it just
something I saw
once on
the CW?

in a way,
I haven't
quite stopped
mourning
the end of my
childhood

People You May Know

27 Mutual Friends
Guy you hooked up with three years ago who treated you like shit.

44 Mutual Friends
Girl you talked to at a party, when she was alone + looked unhappy, who blew you off as soon as her BF came.

does it mean I'm
an adult if I
want to jerk off
to the furniture at
Crate & Barrel ?

the terms
"husband" & "wife"
scare the shit
out of me

VENNTING

WHAT IT FEELS LIKE
TO BE IN YOUR TWENTIES

explanation attempt #7

ATTEMPTING
TO
READ
WINGDINGS

MY FEELINGS
FOR YOU

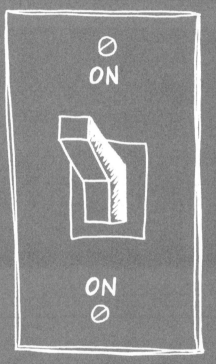

i'm not sure it's even possible for me to stop wanting you.

I'm 99% sure that someone drugged me one night and forced me to sign up for

because I have no memory of ever doing so and now I get tons of meaningless emails from them.

//≡//≡//≡//≡//≡//≡//≡//≡//
RIGHT NOW, I HAVE NO CONCRETE PROOF OF WHAT TRANSPIRED THAT FATEFUL NIGHT, BUT <u>I AM WATCHING YOU, LINKEDIN.</u>
YOU BETTER SLEEP WITH ONE EYE OPEN!!!

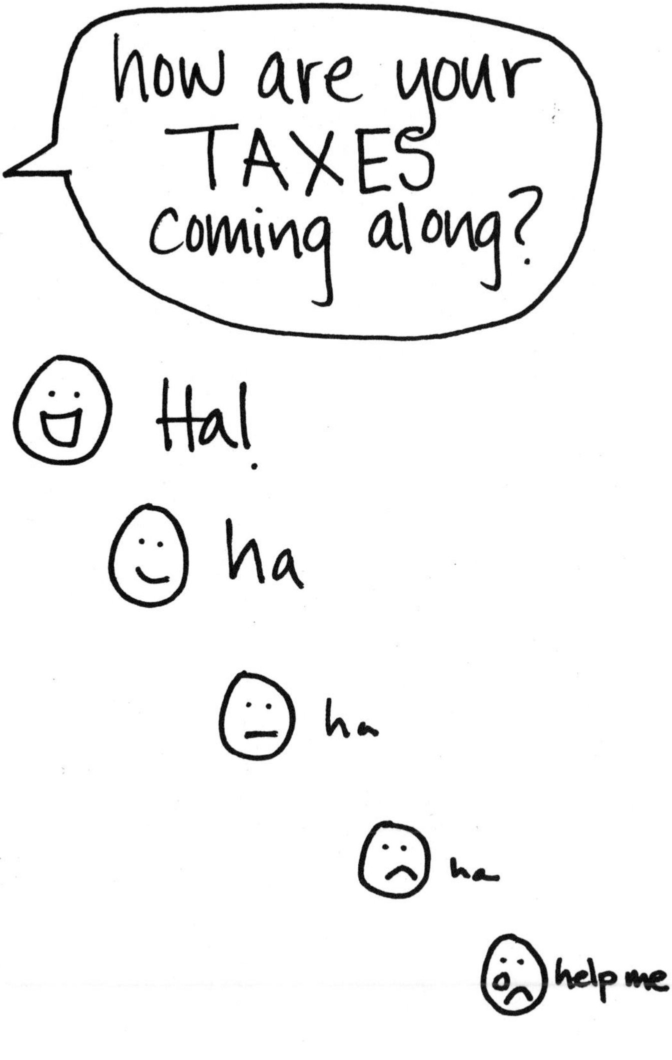
how are your TAXES coming along?
Ha!
ha
ha
ha
help me

WHAT IT FEELS LIKE TO BE IN YOUR TWENTIES

explanation attempt # 8

I look like a **TEEN***

I think like an **ADULT***

I feel like a **KID***

* WHATEVER THE FUCK THOSE
TERMS ACTUALLY MEAN

the all-too-familiar cycle

I am constantly plagued by the immense, intangible weight of my 11,129 unread emails

I DON'T WANT TO BE TOO OLD TO:

1. SLEEP WITH A STUFFED ANIMAL

2. DRESS IN OUTFITS THAT ARE
TOO REVEALING OR TOO
COSTUME-Y OR TOO CASUAL

3. HAVE AN AFFINITY FOR CANDY

4. CRASH AT MY FRIENDS' PLACES
MORE THAN I SLEEP AT MY OWN

5. POWER THROUGH A HANGOVER

friend genogram

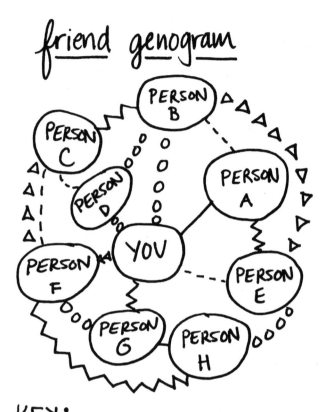

KEY:

———————————→ DATED

– – – – – – → HOOKED UP WITH

∿∿∿∿∿∿∿ → LIVED WITH

▷▷▷▷▷▷▷ → WORKED WITH

o o o o o o o o → WENT TO SCHOOL WITH

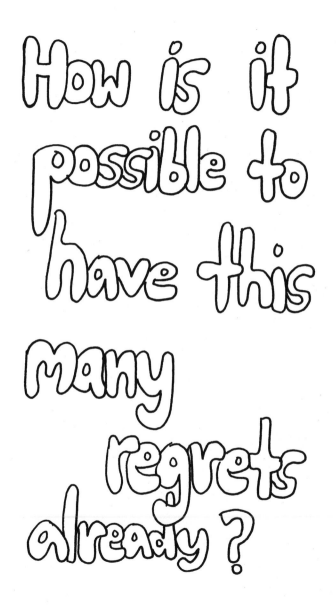

— Yeah, so I'm gonna go.

Which direction are you walking in? We can walk together... cuz I'm, like, leaving, too.

— I'm going south, but I'm in a rush so I should walk alone. I walk faster when I'm alone... Yup... so...

You are weird. —

— Ha. Ok. Whatever.

I'm not sure which was worse: the awkward sex we just had or the awkward conversation I just had with your roommate.

Possible Ways to Greet Someone

Factors to Consider

- polite smile
- smirk
- subtle nod
- wink
- handshake
- fist pound
- high five
- chest bump
- bear hug
- side hug
- hug accompanied by pat on back
- kiss on the cheek
- kiss on both cheeks
- kiss on the mouth
- eskimo kiss
- butterfly kiss
- passionate make-out session
- salute
- bow
- curtsy
- tackle
- spank
- throw a drink in the other's face

- the location
- who else is around
- public vs. private
- sober vs. drunk vs. high
- how long it's been since we've seen each other
- if we missed each other during that period
- if we've met before
- our moods
- is one of us insecure about potential bad breath, excessive sweat, etc.?
- is one of us seated / will prime seating real estate be lost if seated party rises?
- have we hooked up?

When did "hello" become so complicated ?????

Google
"free episodes of law & order"
SEARCH
Did you mean:
"I feel utterly alone"?

Meet this girl.

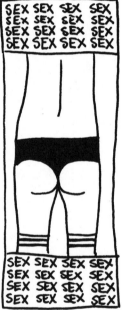

She's an 18-year-old salesperson at our Hell's Kitchen location. In her downtime, this girl enjoys studying heterodox economics, eating patent-leather-flavored popsicles, and wearing hot pink. She's also the star of our first XXX film:

Hot Shorts, High Socks, & Hardcore

American Apparel®

WHAT IT FEELS LIKE TO BE IN YOUR TWENTIES

explanation attempt #9

Sometimes,

the Internet

me

out.

Ooh! I'd LOVE to get lunch with you tomorrow!

The thing is — I don't have a ton of time because I promised myself I'd wake up early and devote an inordinate amount of time to dwelling on my recent regrets.

Then at 1pm, I'm supposed to have a hysterical meltdown cuz I haven't had one in a while and I'm due for one.

So... it looks like I'd really only have a 45-minute window. Hmm... Rain check?

Great! Let's touch base next week!
☺ ☺ ☺ ☺ ☺ ☺ ☺ ☺ ☺ ☺

There should be some kind of loyalty rewards program for getting hurt over and over again

... and then sometimes, when you desperately want the universe to throw you a crumb, you wind up getting a <u>FUCKLOAD OF BREAD!</u>

I'm terrified that one day I'll be having an intimate conversation with someone and a pop-up ad will suddenly appear in front of their face.

Mmm... I know exactly what you mean! Then what happened??

He
and
so I

"Mmm..."? Are you hungry? Sounds like it! Why not try SUPER FUCKTASTIC DORITOS? They taste FUCKTASTIC!

CLICK TO CLOSE ✕

conversation hearts

Yo, it's me! You have my number now!

Yayyy! Now I can finally fulfill my dream of calling u every hr on the hr

That sounds pretty labor-intensive, but I totes admire your commitment

Thnx, boo! But in all seriousness, it was really nice to meet ya

Nice to meet you, too. We should hang soon.

Mos def. Maybe this weekend?

This weekend works for me. I'm thinking we sneak a bottle of Jameson into "The Green Hornet" ?!

You took the words right out of my mouth! Will get in touch later this week :)

WHENEVER I REALLY LIKE SOMEONE, I GO BACK AND READ OUR ENTIRE TEXT MESSAGE EXCHANGE FROM THE BEGINNING (MULTIPLE TIMES)

"I've been worried about you because you haven't been here for a few days. Is everything ok? Is work stressing you out?"

I have more emotionally complex relationships with my usual baristas than I have with some of my friends.

WHAT IT FEELS LIKE TO BE IN YOUR TWENTIES

| explanation attempt #10 |

THE REAL
TIME

WHAT IT
FEELS LIKE

WHAT I WANT
IT TO BE

THE TIME
YOU'RE TELLING
ME IT IS

WHAT IT
FEELS
LIKE NOW

HOW MUCH
TIME I'VE
WASTED

ALL THE DAYS ARE STARTING
TO BLEND TOGETHER

PARANOIA

THROUGH

NUMBERS

APPROXIMATE AMOUNT OF TIMES I CHECK

- that my cell phone is off before a movie — 30
- that I locked my door — 5
- that I am typing your name into the search box and not making it my status — 2
- to make sure my headphones are plugged into my laptop before I start watching porn — 8
- that I unplugged my straightening iron — 3
- my cell phone throughout the day — 500
- my bag for my keys & wallet on a daily basis — 24
- that my fly isn't down — 11
- social networking sites — number too high to accurately compute

 Maybe I can MacGyver an outfit out of pistachio shells, oven mitts, and scotch tape!

WHAT WILL IT TAKE FOR ME TO DO MY LAUNDRY?
(Because lack of clothing to wear is apparently not enough of an incentive)

Things I'm Looking For in A Guy

- super funny & thinks I'm super funny
- highly intelligent
- attractive to the point of being irresistible
- loyal
- great at communicating

~~[all crossed out]~~

- super funny
- fairly smart (quasi-decent)
- ~~good looking~~ ~~decent~~ looking
- there's more than a 60% chance he won't cheat
- will communicate when prompted

~~[all crossed out]~~

- has super funny friends
- has read more than 1 ~~book~~ magazine in the past decade
- ~~I'm not repulsed by the sight of him~~
- ~~can speak in full sentences~~
  (monosyllabic replies & expressive eyes = OK)
- has cheated on me, ~~but still ranks me as #1~~ ← ranking not <u>that</u> important

- doesn't totally embarrass me   ✓ YES!
- ~~lives near a lot of subway lines~~
- has air conditioning !!!

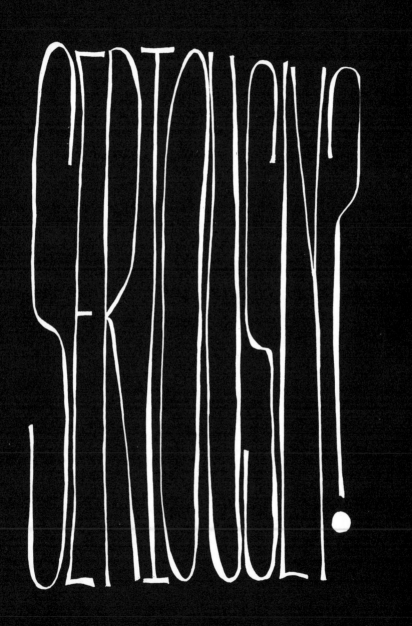

IN THE FOLLOWING YEAR,
I AM ALMOST CERTAIN
THAT I WILL:

- DO SOMETHING THAT MANY PEOPLE HAVE ADVISED ME NOT TO DO
- SLEEP THROUGH MY ALARM AND WAKE UP IN A PANIC
- DEVELOP A CRUSH ON SOMEONE UNATTAINABLE AND IT WILL EAT ME UP INSIDE
- HAVE VERY UNSATISFYING SEX
- AGREE TO SOMETHING I DON'T WANT TO OUT OF GUILT
- BE REJECTED
- COMPLAIN ABOUT HOW IT IS TOO HOT OR TOO COLD
- FIND WAYS TO JUSTIFY THE POOR DECISIONS I WILL END UP MAKING
- HAVE MANY NIGHTS WHERE I WON'T BE ABLE TO FALL ASLEEP
- BE SEXUALLY HARRASSED AND/OR INSULTED BY STRANGERS ON THE STREET
- DOUBT MYSELF TREMENDOUSLY
- HAVE MANY CONVERSATIONS THAT ARE SAD or FRUSTRATING or UNCOMFORTABLE or ALL 3
- GET MOSQUITO BITES AND HEADACHES AND COLDS AND SUFFER FROM ALLERGIES
- FEEL LIKE AN IDIOT
- BE BETRAYED
- WORRY ABOUT MAKING ENOUGH MONEY

but... it will be okay.

FRONT

Greetings from the future!

BACK

2/6/2030

Dear You,

Wish you were here! Remember that you are doing just fine!

Best Wishes,
Future You

$10

My Younger
Self